The BRIDAL Changing Room

LISA HARTELL

The Bridal Changing Room

The BRIDAL Changing Room

Copyright © 2007
by Lisa Hartell
All Rights Reserved.

No part of this publication may be reproduced, stored in a retrieval system, or transmitted in any form or by any means – electronic, mechanical, photocopy, recording, or any other – without the prior permission of the publisher.

All Scripture quotations, unless otherwise indicated, are taken from the Holy Bible, New King James Version. Copyright © 1982 by Thomas Nelson, Inc. Used by permission. All rights reserved.

ISBN 978-0-9749234-1-9

Cover photo of Melissa Emmerson used with permission.

The Bridal Changing Room

*I dedicate these pages
To my sons,
Andrew and Austin ~*

*"You are part of the beautiful Bride of Christ.
God uses you powerfully,
uniquely
and joyously.*

*Your quest with Jesus
is the most exciting adventure
in all of creation.
Like a Bridegroom to His Lover,
He pursues you daily,
drawing you continually to Himself
with His extravagant loving kindness."*

The Bridal Changing Room

Acknowledgements

Andy - My husband, my love, my friend. Thank you for your unconditional love and encouragement to be all God wants me to be, as unique as I am. You, along with the way Your Heavenly Father made you, are a gift being continually unwrapped and presented by Jesus. I love the way He makes us 'one'.

Joe Edwards ~ Your passion for Christ and the Word of God made your editing a gift from the Father to this work. The spirit of Truth through you is mighty! Your love for Christ and His body are even more! Thank you for your contribution and encouragement - it is a privilege and blessing to labor in the fields with you, dear brother.

Victor Badilla ~ Your obedience to the Lord to translate this work into Spanish will bring forth great fruit in the Kingdom. You too are a beautiful part of His bride. Thank You for allowing Him to use you so greatly, so faithfully, to reach the lost, and to bless my life. You are a joy to have as a brother in Christ and friend.

Ann Martinec – Prayer partnerships are birthed out of the heart of Jesus. We have Him in common. Your gift of faith was God's plan to bless me most in the hours I was being bombarded with trial and tribulation in an endeavor to move forward in my own growth in answering the call to write and speak what He gives me. God uses it all to mold Jesus in our hearts. You are my sister for eternity. I thank God for you.

Linda – My sister. My friend. God knew.

The Bridal Changing Room

Introduction

I never intend to write what I write. Nor did I ever imagine or set out to be an author or one who shares her experiences with God. All my efforts of producing anything of value and impact came to naught, when I collapsed in the arms of Jesus many moons ago. I was tired, frustrated, despaired from "trying" to make something of my life. Somehow, my life had gotten off track from my childhood decision to trust Him as my Savior and Lord. I had found myself on the dreadful treadmill of working to be good enough and acceptable in His sight.

Everything began to flow freely the moment My Jesus whispered to me, "That's right – just give up [trying]…you can't do it – I must do it through you." It was the most priceless golden mystery that had ever been revealed to me. I had to learn – like the rest of mankind, "The Way" into the Kingdom of God is not through anything I can do in my strength – but through total surrender – just as Jesus let the life of the Father flow through Him.

With that, My Jesus picked up the myriad of pieces of my desperate and wearied soul and began to live His life fully through me. Piece by piece He has continued putting me back together – preparing me for our Wedding Day.

He filled my every breath and poured His spirit in, until I thought my body would explode from the glory of Him – and He did this again and again – as often as I would return to that quiet and still place of total surrender. It became my life – to come and rest in Him. I began to understand what it meant to drink of the living water – and to eat of the bread of Life. His life flowing through me was changing me. It was all I could do, to find words to begin to describe what He had done in the deepest places of my heart. My writing and expression of words and living, became filled with life and passionate purpose.

The world around me changed. Not in appearance …but in the way I viewed it. I began to see the glory of God everywhere. On my morning walks upon the corn fields that were sprinkled with dew and glistening in the warm radiance. In the eyes of my children. Upon my husband, standing across the room…upon the woman in front of me while waiting in line to purchase food for my family. I had finally begun to see that the Kingdom of God was at hand – in my own life.

It was after that, that my passion for writing increased and began to change. Poetry that I once used to painstakingly write *about* Him, became expressions of my experiences *with* Him using a pen and paper. Writing and speaking were tools that I once used to express my desperate need to be filled by Him. After that revelatory moment, my writing became a blessed tool to express the overflow of what He had poured in. I became keenly aware that the Jesus in me, had plans, desires and work that He wanted to accomplish using my hands, heart, words, and gifts. Later, He commissioned me to write, "The Mom Ministry," my first book. Then another

The Bridal Changing Room

work and another work, until the day He unveiled this piece from His heart ~

The Bridal Changing Room

I do not claim this writing is anything more than what I saw on the screen of my heart and mind, when I sat down with Him that warm summer day.

Though I remember that day distinctly, the river of inspiration seemed to overtake me, and before I could fully realize what was happening, I was drawn to the computer like a fish out of water is drawn to the ocean…and typing faster than ever.

I remember His Presence, still. His satisfying and saturating Presence ~ was rich in the room. As I wrote, every cell in my being felt as if it were filled with electric oxygen, tears rolled down my cheeks at the words that came flowing onto the pages. In little over 1 hour – this work was complete from start to finish, with only minor typographical errors and a few repeated adjectives that were changed to spare you the redundancy. You are reading it, almost untouched and unaltered, with the exception of layout and cover design. My prayer is that, you will be blessed as you read and share it with others. My hope and prayer above all is that as you read, you too will experience the same presence and grace that I did, the day it was written.

It's not an accident you happened to pick up this book to read today. God is sovereignly at work all around you – in this very moment to reveal Himself to you. His intention through every sunray, breeze blowing, wave that crashes and star that falls, is to get your attention. To cause you to lift your eyes – and realize – It's HIM! Watching, waiting for and loving you with endless passion.

He desires to touch and fill you – again and again. As you read and experience His heart for you and those around you? Just thank Him for it and realize it's Him warming your soul – not eloquent words. He wants to be near you, heal you, refresh you and Yes, He will use you – but not to the fullest, until you have discovered the freedom in His unconditional love for you.

He loves you with an unending passion –
and He made you to know it!

For the Praise and Glory of Our Loving King,

- Lisa Hartell

The Bridal Changing Room

Feeling lifted up, almost as if I was standing in mid air, I looked and there before me was a beautiful bride standing near the opening of an old ancient doorway. As my vision expanded to a wider view, I could see that she was one of many brides, carrying the same heart. Each was stationed at their own uniquely appointed place.

My attention was drawn to the one before me who was adorned in the most beautiful bridal gown I had ever seen. It was an exquisite scene. As I panned my view from right to left, each bride was perfectly extraordinary (beautiful in her own special way). Each one was so completely beautiful and different, it was impossible to tell which one was more exquisite.

Streaming through each ancient doorway was brilliant light. Of such tranquility and majesty, there are no earthly words to describe. The light was "experiential dancing light" (the kind that fills your entire being and all of heaven and earth with it). In it every emotion, thought, and sense you have feels as if you are "one" with all of God's heart, mind, and creation – it is the sense of perfect order from eternity past to eternity future. A feeling one can never forget. The light made the bride's dresses shimmer and glisten almost as if the dresses themselves had come to life. Each one was radiant and a brighter white than I had ever seen with my earthly eyes. Like brand new contacts or eye glasses after a long season of blurred vision, my sight became crystal clear and perfect. I could see for what seemed like thousands of miles, and then even farther into what seemed like thousands of years and into eternity. "I never want to leave this place," I thought.

The light radiating through each old rugged doorway was perfectly pure. Deep inside, I knew it was the glory of God. The glory-light was alive and was filled with purpose. It was a substance that changed everything it touched and fell upon. The light was filled with movement and energy that brought hope and lift to my spirit and entire being. I wanted to stay there and never move again, absorbing its warmth and vitality.

Until behind me, I heard the sound of something so different than what I was now experiencing. It left me feeling deeply disturbed in my spirit. With the sound, came

The Bridal Changing Room

an unbelievable weight of heaviness to my heart – that made it painful to listen to. My attention was so fixed and drawn into the light I had been enjoying, that it was difficult to turn away from it. But something inside drew me to do so. My head began to turn toward this awful sound without another thought.

As I turned I looked over my left shoulder. I remember struggling as the sound increased. In the next moment, shock (like lightning) struck my heart at the first glimpse. I could hardly believe what I was seeing. The pain in my heart filled me until my tongue became thick and unable to speak. Heaviness enveloped me until I felt I couldn't stand anymore at the sight. Frozen and in amazement I stood, while there before me was an outstretched mass of crawling, agonizing bodies.

The numbers of them were more than I've ever seen in my life or could have imagined. Covered in what seemed like a shroud of darkness that you could feel with your hands and every sense in your body, the moving mass of bodies stretched as far as the eye could see. Most were on their bellies, crawling and doing all they could to continue to move forward. They were coming in my direction. They were moving with all their strength towards the ancient doorways near the place I was standing. The contrast between the beauty of the light of the glory and the darkened agony and gloom – was like night and day.

Without realizing it, my mouth had begun to move effortlessly, and I could hear myself breathing the words, "Oh Jesus…Oh Jesus…Dear Jesus…".

They were like a sea of crushed warriors, who were crawling army-style, some had managed to make it up onto their knees with heads hanging low. Every movement was a struggle for them. They had been bloodied, beaten, raped, tormented, with their filthy clothes torn and barely hanging from their bodies. They had no strength to walk…it looked like the after-affects of a bloody war scene.

In my heart the following words came to my understanding,

"These are they that are being called out of darkness".

Many had given up along the way and felt unable to continue on in their journey. Each was trying desperately to muster up the strength to continue to press forward. Some had completely given up to die and were laying there barely able to breathe, while others crawled over them – straining to draw nearer. They were too weak, wounded, and sick to be able to help one another. To survive, they had shifted into an "every man for himself"- mentality.

The battle to come out of darkness was fierce – literally, life or death. The enemy of their souls had not only lured them, but had stripped and tormented them; leaving

The Bridal Changing Room

them with nothing but the seeds of faith they were once given.

Leaving the darkness cost them everything they had. All they had left was each seed that had been planted deep within their heart and spirit, in the secret place where the evil one is not allowed to tread.

It is the seed of their destiny that remains alive and serves as a container for words of encouragement to keep crawling. The life in each seed was what was now keeping them alive. Their only hope was to keep moving forward, pressing toward the light. The darkness pulled at them continually to turn back.

The mass continued crawling slowly towards the light. In the distance I could hear the sound of the brides standing at the doorway to the Kingdom.

The crawling warriors, who had eyes open enough to see, saw the glory light ahead in the distance – it was drawing them and feeding them life and strength to keep pressing forward.

Over the sound of the agonizing mass of people, I heard a beautiful sound in the distance. The beautiful sound was increasing in its intensity and volume, and my ears quickly tuned in. It brought me comfort to listen. I had begun to feel heavy at the sound of the groaning mass of people. As I tuned in and turned toward the light, it seemed to get louder and easier to hear. It was the sound of many voices...it was the sound of the bride, calling forth the masses of people who were struggling to come out of the darkness & despair.

The voices of the Bride began to lift and were carried high above their cries, weeping and groaning. Their voices began to blend, yet carried a distinct and unique beauty just as each of their bridal gowns had. Some at the doorways were new at using their voice and were learning to blend and make their beautiful sound with the others. Others more mature in using their voice, had the sound of added grace and smoothness in the spirit.

Along with each unique beautiful sound, came a rich substance flowing from it – rich and sweet like honey. It was the presence of hope, faith and love – wrapped in the Word of God. It acted as food for the soul, medicine for wounds, and bread of life and encouragement to all who could hear.

As the bride opened her mouth and shouted, spoke, sang and prayed, strength to continue the journey was released to the struggling crawlers. Each word or note of music enabled them to continue to move forward towards the light. Carried by the Spirit, the sound filled the air above, opening the heavens, almost creating a way in the skies for the light of glory to come through.

There were brides that were anointed to reach those close by, and yet other brides had the God-given ability to lift a voice that would be carried to those a far off. Each one was learning to speak, write, sing, dance, and use their voice and gifts skillfully and with all of their purified heart. They

The Bridal Changing Room

desired deeply for Jesus to receive His bride; those who are now, and those who are yet to come. Only then, can His heart be fully satisfied.

I walked into the glory room, and saw Jesus singing and speaking – He had become ONE with the heart of His bride. It was His very voice emanating through them. They cried out to prepare the way of the Lord.

I heard the voice of one crawler who had begun to cry and talk to herself in utter defeat, "I can't make it anymore, it's too far, I can't make it…" she wept as she laid her head down one more time, knowing she couldn't lift another muscle to continue one more moment.

Just then, I heard the sound of one of the brides in a doorway call out, "You can make it…don't give up". She had heard the voice of the hopeless crawler from afar, and prayed, "Lord, send your Spirit to give her strength…she wants you, help her draw near".

In that moment, the very spirit-strength that was needed drew the despairing struggler one more time. I saw clearly that every prayer, every word or song of life coming forth is critical for each of the struggling warriors to crawl out of the darkness.

BEYOND THE DOOR
THE CHANGING ROOM

The sea of crawlers were covered in dark, dirty, torn and ragged clothes, some of them had lost shoes along the way, some had feet that were bloodied from their journey, and they were so very tired of trying to make it through.

I heard the sound of the bride calling out, each one had a unique sound in her voice – yet, spoke in unity and harmony with the heart of the Father. The uniqueness of their own special way of crying out and calling forth the sea of people was a wonder to behold, as I could see the endless creativity of God being displayed through each of them. Their voices blended like a rainbow of colors flowing one right into the other ~ another wonder to behold. I understood more than ever before, that we, while strikingly unique as individuals were created to flow together, and be fully who we are in Christ so that His living light and glory can stream through us and illuminate to the world His splendor and presence.

In between breaths I saw the bride praying at each of the doorways. They prayed intensely and wholeheartedly for the weary travelers. I turned and saw one bride with tears streaming down her cheeks, struggling to hold back her sobs for them. Like the other brides, her heart had been broken for them…she had been talking to Jesus in between her messages

The Bridal Changing Room

to the struggling crawlers. In a heartfelt whisper, and amidst all the millions of voices, Jesus could hear her perfectly. He was near her, standing behind her in the light of the Glory beyond the doorway where she was stationed. She said to Him, "They're coming, Jesus. Your bride is coming..." she whispered..."aren't you happy? They're coming to you...look, even now, many are entering the doorway."

This touched my heart so deeply with wonder and amazement. It was odd to hear her call the crawling warriors, "the BRIDE," as she spoke to Jesus. They didn't look at all like she did. They were covered in dirt, filth and wore clothes that gave off a rotten stench from all the garbage they had crawled through on their journey...yet she distinctly referred to them as 'Your bride'.

My heart was drawing me to walk through the doorway that I was standing in. The light was so bright, however, I couldn't see what was in it - or who? I knew that the light was the presence of Jesus and that was enough for me to step through, by faith, without seeing beyond to where it would lead me. I stepped through. Nothing could have prepared me for the glorious experience I was about to have.

In a moment, a sensation of standing under a waterfall of light had flooded my being. I knew it was another realm of heaven that was filled with transformation for all those who continue to make the choice to press in. It had been prepared for each one who continually says "no" to the world, and says "I want more of You, Lord; I want to know you deeply, and with my whole being". Only those who had been washed in the blood, and had said "Yes" to Him, were led to this place in His presence. It was the place where eternal change and His glory consume our being. No other requirements were necessary, except simple child-like faith that leads to obedience and a desire to know and love Him more. This was the key to stepping forward and obtaining more of Him.

The Bridal Changing Room

THE GOWN

As I gazed over my shoulder, I was drawn once again to the light of His glory. I began to make my way toward the doorway, when for a split second I noticed a sparkle and flash of light beneath me. I looked down and discovered I too had been standing in a beautiful wedding gown. How could I have not noticed before this moment, that I too was adorned in such a beautiful gown? The change of clothing had brought a great change in my heart and soul. The covering of His complete love, and His acceptance of every part of me along with the freedom that was received from Him, led to deeper levels of joy welling up into righteousness in every area of my life. Yet I wasn't aware until this moment, how beautiful He had dressed me in the spirit. In that moment, I realized our lives and experiences are preparation for eternity with our Bridegroom.

As I looked more closely at my gown, I saw that it was detailed with pearls, diamonds, and stones I had never seen before. They were perfectly fashioned onto perfect white linen...it was like nothing I had ever seen or imagined before. Yet, it felt so ordinary, so relaxing and comfortable, for a bridal gown. It felt as if it was made just for me, not stiff and "new" like I remember the bridal gown I wore on my own earthly wedding day. This felt more comfortable and custom-fitted than my favorite pajamas. It actually felt alive with life and warmth. Yet, my heart and mind kept returning to the sea of others behind me, agonizing to move forward out of the darkness. I began to ache inside for them to have the same gift.

I knew my destiny was beyond the ancient door ~ the bride of Christ, and calling forth those destined for the Kingdom into His glory, including our own children and families. The glory we bask in, when we seek His face, is for purpose. It's used to fill us with His very life and spirit so that when we speak, sing, pray and "Go", our voice and life will be ONE with Father, Son and Holy Spirit, and emanate their heart and life. Only when we are saturated with His presence can we be used by Him to bring strength to the war-torn strugglers, who are yearning to crawl out of the darkness and into the fellowship of His light. Whether our individual voice carries near or far, we must each lift our voices, uniquely and with all our might…reaching every one who will listen. It's their only hope.

I cried as I turned to look back at the moving mass of strugglers. Looking back at them now, for the first time I was able to see what I must have looked like crawling out of the darkness myself. Though it was so long ago, it felt like yesterday as I looked on. I could feel their anguish in deep sympathy and concern for them. I felt a lump rising in my throat, remembering the depression I once experienced, the thoughts of insanity that I had once battled, the constant feelings that no one liked me, the voices I heard in the night telling me to give up, feeling I would never make it or ever be more than a worthless piece of garbage. I was looking at a picture of where I and every other member of the bride of Christ had come from.

The Bridal Changing Room

At the sight of the mass before me, a burning fire began to rise up in my belly – one that filled my chest. It was a surge of unction that I had never felt at this level of intensity before. I struggled to contain it, to keep myself composed, but something powerful welled up within me that began to fill my lungs and overtake me. With a moment of decision to let it come forth, it felt as if a damn had broken and an ocean of love and desperation gushed forth as I lifted my chin, my voice and with my entire being began to cry out,

"**Come…You can make it.
Don't give up!
IT'S TIME TO COME HOME –
into the Light.
There's a brand new bridal gown waiting for you –
garments of white – His righteousness. His glory light to adorn you – His joy to lift you.
YOU WERE DESTINED FOR THE
LIGHT – don't turn back…**"

The cry went forth, and it was heard by the struggling crawlers. At the sound, the spirit words filled them with enough strength to continue moving forward, toward the great ancient doorways. The masses were moving forward, forward, struggling to press forward. Hearing the sound of my voice made those with a past similar to my own listen intently to the hope that was being carried to their spiritual ears and hearts. Others in the mass were drawn to the other brides with a similar past experience, finding strength to overcome their own hindrances and press forward toward more of the radiant dancing light.

Many had already made it and crossed over the threshold, leaving behind even more faith and hope for the others that were coming behind them. Once inside, a most glorious sight and experience awaited them.

THE ROOM

I turned to follow one bride in, beyond the ancient door. She had used every ounce of faith she had to cross over the last few hurdles. Angels had been working on her behalf to help her forward and step in.

To be beyond the door, was beyond comprehension, as I watched her close her eyes and rest for the first time in her life. I felt her heart, flooded with emotion say, "home, it feels like I'm home," she muttered with lips barely moving, as a tender child-like smile curved across her small, cracked and broken lips.

Angels, filled with joy, ministered to her. Attendants, glowing in white, had come immediately carrying her own personal gown, serving her with living water and the bread of life that nourished her tired and weary soul.

She found supernatural replenishment and strength with every moment, cleansing from a sponge of Jesus blood that washed away every impure and lying thought that had once clouded her mind. I watched her sit up and begin to beam with radiant light. The angels helped her to her feet, holding her ankles as they began to change her shoes, then her torn and filthy clothes – it was time for the changing of her garments.

As I watched, I found myself reminiscing back to the time of my own crossing over. The joy of that moment filled my heart, soul, and body once again as I turned and entered in ~ the glory light filled me once again. Sheer delight consumed me, along with hope and joy beyond all comprehension. To my left I saw a heap of clothes, heaped almost to the ceiling, that were too many to count. They were the clothes that had been removed here in the Bridal Changing Room.

Old, dark, filthy, torn, and smoldering, they were awaiting their removal into the fire, where they would never be seen or worn again. There were angels coming and going, hauling them away. There was such joy in their work as they knew each item they carried away represented another soul receiving their eternal wardrobe – garments of white, exactly to the Kings liking.

As I stepped further into the bridal changing room, to my right, my mind couldn't comprehend the greatness of what I was about to behold. There were uncountable souls being helped into their new bridal gowns. Each one was completely unique and being assisted in the careful positioning of her dress. Those assisting were filled with happiness and songs of joy for the one who was being fitted. It was like watching a newborn baby coming forth. The moment of her dreams had come true – she had finally stepped into who she was destined to be. A bride ~ being prepared to dance and romance with her King ~ not a mere fairy tale, but a real life romance with the King of all Kings – Jesus.

There would be much preparation for the wedding night that's ahead. There were many in place to help prepare

The Bridal Changing Room

them – but many more were needed and were being called to step forward out of their preparation rooms. The masses were coming in at a rapid rate of speed. And time was short.

As I walked behind the brides who were being changed into their wedding gowns, I saw another door towards the back of the room. I was drawn to it. Rugged, heavy and cracked open just a bit, it was as if I was being pulled to approach it and walk beyond its huge archway. It seemed familiar to me; a sense draped over me that I had walked that way before. Slowly my memory began to clear, and I remembered the day I had wept at the feet of Jesus in prayer – it was the day long ago He had called me into His work. I remembered feeling God's presence descend upon me in my living room so long ago. The weight of it pressed me to the floor in humility like I had never known before. I struggled to get lower and lower as I whispered to My Father-God, "I surrender, I surrender, I surrender to you…".

That was the day He called me to lift my voice as a vessel for Him… the day He laid His hand upon me to call forth this generation. The many brides were waiting to receive their bridal gowns, but needed encouragement to come forth.

In that moment, I realized, the holy experience I had that day in the natural was real in the Kingdom of Heaven. The place in the spirit that I was now standing in was the door to trumpet His message and His voice, to all who would hear it. Though I was in my living room on the floor in prayer that day, I was literally in a heavenly place in the spirit at the very same time. It was an awesome realization that I was standing at the very doorway where I embraced my calling.

As I passed through, the desire to crumble to my knees overtook me once again. The desire to weep for the weight of His Holy Presence swept over me. "Yes, receive added strength and a renewed touch of My Spirit. Come here and be renewed, when the strain of your journey wearies you," Jesus said. "I lead you daily. It is My presence that led you to this door the very first time. It is My meeting place with you. Do so each time you need to revisit the place where you were first commissioned. Call forth this generation, both great and small, young and old".

"My love and spirit lead you each day," He continued, "when you find yourself overwhelmed, weary, tired, and ready to give up, turn to Me, call on My name, and I will strengthen you."

Passing through the open door, I was led to the outside of the building, where I found a brown dirt path suddenly beneath my feet. The glory light illuminated its path and led me back to the place where I began. Walking, walking onward along the edge of the building, around the side of the building, I walked till I began to hear the sound of the agonizing crawlers again – in minutes I found myself nearing the front of the glorious building. Turning to my right I saw the ancient doorways once again, and the brides standing at each doorway (each still heralding their message of hope to the struggling crawlers). There was a doorway standing open, and I knew it was mine…awaiting my return

The Bridal Changing Room

to take my place in the Kingdom and lift my voice once again.

My heart swelled with gratefulness for the renewed strength and vigor I had found only moments earlier on my journey through the bridal changing room and by revisiting the door way of my calling with Jesus. It was the very presence of Christ in each of those places that had filled me with renewed hope and strength to carry on.

From behind me, I heard the sound of a roaring lion echoing through all of heaven. Its sound filled the atmosphere, causing all that was in heaven and under it to thunder and quake. From in the midst of it was the sound of a voice like many waters flowing endlessly that said, "Go, into all the world and preach the gospel to every creature….the time is short…"

Revelation 21:9-11, 22-27

"Then one of the seven angels who had the seven bowls filled with the seven last plagues came to me and talked with me, saying,

**"Come, I will show you the bride,
the Lamb's wife."**

And he carried me away in the Spirit to a great and high mountain, and showed me the great city, the holy Jerusalem, descending out of heaven from God, having the glory of God.
Her light was like a most precious stone, like a jasper stone, clear as crystal...

But I saw no temple in it, for the Lord God Almighty and the Lamb are its temple. The city had no need of the sun or of the moon to shine in it, for the glory of God illuminated it. The Lamb is its light. And the nations of those who are saved shall walk in its light, and the kings of the earth
bring their glory and honor into it.
It's gates shall not be shut at all by day
(there shall be no night there).
And they shall bring the glory and the honor of the nations into it.
But there shall by no means enter it anything that defiles, or causes an abomination or a lie, but only those who are written in
the Lamb's Book of Life.

The Bridal Changing Room

Revelation 21:2-4

"Then, I, John, saw the holy city, New Jerusalem, coming down out of heaven from God, prepared as a bride adorned for her husband.

And I heard a loud voice from heaven saying, "Behold, the tabernacle of God is with men, and He will dwell with them, and they shall be His people. God Himself will be with them and be their God.

And God will wipe away every tear from their eyes; there shall be no more death, nor sorrow, nor crying. There shall be no more pain, for the former things have passed away."

I Peter 2:4-12

As you come to him, the living Stone – rejected by men but chosen by God and precious to him you also like living stones, are being built into a spiritual house to be a holy priesthood, offering spiritual sacrifices acceptable to God through Jesus Christ.
For in Scripture it says:
"See, I lay a stone in Zion,
A chosen and precious Cornerstone,

And the one who trusts in him
Will never be put to shame."
Now to you who believe, this stone is precious. But to those who do not believe,
"The stone the builders rejected
Has become the capstone,
And "A stone that causes men to stumble
And a rock that makes them fall."

They stumble because they disobey the message – which is also what they were destined for.

But you are a chosen people,
A royal priesthood, a holy nation, a people belonging to God,
that you may declare the praises of him who called you out of the darkness into his wonderful light.

Once you were not a people, but now
you are the people of God;
once you had not received mercy,
but now you have received mercy.

Dear friends, I urge you, as aliens
and strangers in the world,
to abstain from sinful desires,
which war against your soul.
Live such good lives among the pagans that, though they accuse you of doing wrong, they may see your good deeds and glorify God on the day he visits us.

The Bridal Changing Room

Revelation 22:12-17

"Behold, I am coming soon!
My reward is with me, and I will give to everyone
according to what he has done. I am the Alpha and the
Omega, the first and the Last,
the Beginning and the End.
Blessed are those who wash their robes, that they may
have the right to the tree of life and may go through the
gates into the city.
Outside are the dogs, those who practice magic arts,
the sexually immoral, the murders, the idolaters and
everyone who loves and practices falsehood.

I, Jesus, have sent my angel to give
you this testimony for the churches. I am the Root and
the Offspring of David, and the bright Morning Star.

The Spirit and the bride say, "Come!" And let him who
hears say, "Come!" Whoever is thirsty, let him come;
And whoever wishes, let him take the free gift of the
water of life.

John 14:12

"...I say to you, he who believes in Me,...greater works
than these he will do, because I go to My Father."

About the Author

Lisa Hartell, along with her husband Andy, are co-founders of *Ignite Ministries International*, a ministry dedicated to bringing relevant biblical teaching with life-changing results to the spiritually hungry and needy. Answering the call of God which she received as a child, Lisa equips the body of Christ and ministers locally and internationally through inspired ministering of the Word of God in Conferences, Special Events, and various organizations. In addition, Lisa also serves the Lord through intercessory prayer. Her passion is to see hearts ignited with the fire of Jesus' presence, so that each may be freed, restored, empowered, equipped, and activated to fulfill the Great Commission.

Lisa's testimony is one of incredible defeat and victory – which God uses to inspire the weary, pull at the strings of the wandering heart, and inspire the complacent to seek His face more than anything in life. Filled with God's grace for the wayward and prodigals, truth for freedom to the bound, and comfort with a healing balm to the bruised and broken; her testimony releases fresh faith, vision and God's life-changing power for your every day life and most hopeless-looking struggles.

"It's not ministry, until Jesus changes your heart,"
Lisa shares.

Lisa's favorite ministry is the one to her family, with Andy, Andrew and AJ (Austin) their two sons. They serve the Lord and were commissioned for global ministry through their local church where they are grounded in covenant relationship. Together, they make their home in Crystal Lake, Illinois.

The Bridal Changing Room

To Host a Life Changing Gathering

in your area
Where You Experience the Presence of God

Any of our books, CDs, or DVD topics are available in
Conference, Workshop, Retreat settings
or in special event formats

To inquire, please Contact our Office ~
or visit

www.TheMomMinistry.com

We are here to serve You!

Ignite Ministries International
Office

Phone: 815-301-7009 / 815-788-8177
Email: igniteministries@sbcglobal.net

Mailing Address:
Ignite Ministries International
PO BOX 132, Crystal Lake, IL   60039-0132

The Bridal Changing Room

ALSO AVAILABLE

Book Series
The Mom Ministry
The Mom Ministry Workshop & Study Guide – Student Edition
The Mom Ministry Workshop & Study Guide – Instructor's Edition
Protecting this Generation from the Spirit of Anti-Christ
The Bridal Changing Room

(All of the above titles Available in Spanish)

Audio CD
Isaiah 61

Audio Cassette
Protecting This Generation from the Spirit of Anti-Christ
Releasing the Power of God in our Home

DVD
Mothers & Fathers in the Spirit – Builders in the Kingdom

To Order or Visit us
www.TheMomMinistry.com

or

www.ignite-ministries.org

The Bridal Changing Room

www.TheMomMinistry.com

The Bridal Changing Room

The Bridal Changing Room